New Careers for the
21st Century:
Finding Your Role in
the Global Renewal

TOMORROW'S TEACHERS:

URBAN LEADERSHIP,

EMPOWERING STUDENTS &

IMPROVING LIVES

New Careers for the 21st Century: Finding Your Role in the Global Renewal

New Careers for the 21st Century: Finding Your Role in the Global Renewal

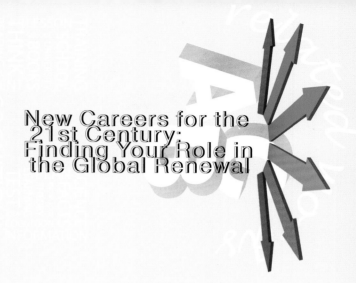

TOMORROW'S TEACHERS:

URBAN LEADERSHIP, EMPOWERING STUDENTS & IMPROVING LIVES

by Malinda Miller

Mason Crest Publishers

TOMORROW'S TEACHERS:

URBAN LEADERSHIP, EMPOWERING STUDENTS & IMPROVING LIVES

MASON CREST PUBLISHERS INC.
370 Reed Road
Broomall, Pennsylvania 19008
(866)MCP-BOOK (toll free)
www.masoncrest.com

First Printing
9 8 7 6 5 4 3 2 1

Library of Congress Cataloging-in-Publication Data

Miller, Malinda, 1979-
Tomorrow's teachers : empowering students & improving lives / by
   Malinda Miller.
      p. cm. — (New careers for the 21st century)
   ISBN 978-1-4222-1823-5   ISBN 978-1-4222-1811-2 (series)
   ISBN 978-1-4222-2044-3 (ppb)   ISBN 978-1-4222-2032-0 (series ppb)
   1. Teaching—Vocational guidance—Juvenile literature. 2. Effective
   teaching—Juvenile literature. 3. Academic achievement—Juvenile
   literature. I. Title.
   LB1775.M55 2011
   371.10023—dc22

                                    2010021832

Produced by Harding House Publishing Service, Inc.
www.hardinghousepages.com
Interior design by MK Bassett-Harvey.
Cover design by Torque Advertising + Design.
Printed in USA by Bang Printing.

CONTENTS

INTRODUCTION

Be careful as you begin to plan your career.

To get yourself in the best position to begin the career of your dreams, you need to know what the "green world" will look like and what jobs will be created and what jobs will become obsolete. Just think, according to the Bureau of Labor Statistics, the following jobs are expected to severely decline by 2012:

- word processors and data-entry keyers
- stock clerks and order fillers
- secretaries
- electrical and electronic equipment assemblers
- computer operators
- telephone operators
- postal service mail sorters and processing-machine operators
- travel agents

These are just a few of the positions that will decrease or become obsolete as we move forward into the century.

You need to know what the future jobs will be. How do you find them? One way is to look where money is being invested. Many firms and corporations are now making investments in startup and research enterprises. These companies may become the "Microsoft" and "Apple" of the twenty-first century. Look at what is being researched and what technology is needed to obtain the results.

Green world, green economy, green technology—they all say the same things: the way we do business today is changing. Every industry will be shaped by the world's new focus on creating a sustainable lifestyle, one that won't deplete our natural and economic resources.

The possibilities are unlimited. Almost any area that will conserve energy and reduce the dependency on fossil fuels is open to new and exciting career paths. Many of these positions have not even been identified yet and will only come to light as the technology progresses and new discoveries are made in the way we use that technology. And the best part about this is that our government is behind us. The U.S. government wants to help you get the education and training you'll need to succeed and grow in this new and changing economy. The U.S. Department of Labor has launched a series of initiatives to support and promote green job creation. To view the report, visit: www.dol.gov/dol/green/ earthday_reportA.pdf.

The time to decide on your future is now. This series, NEW CAREERS FOR THE 21ST CENTURY: FINDING YOUR ROLE IN THE GLOBAL RENEWAL, can act as the first step toward your continued education, training, and career path decisions. Take the first steps that will lead you—and the planet—to a productive and sustainable future.

Mike Puglisi
Department of Labor, District I Director (New York/New Jersey)
IAWP (International Association of Workforce Professionals)

The essence of teaching is to make learning contagious, to have one idea spark another.

—Marva Collins

ABOUT THE QUOTE

Do you enjoy learning? Are you curious about the world around you? Do you get excited about new ideas? These attitudes could help you become the kind of teacher who inspires your students to learn.

CHAPTER 1
THE IMPORTANCE OF TEACHERS

WORDS TO KNOW

vocational: Having to do with education that is focused on a certain occupation and its skills.
tactile: Connected to the sense of touch.
kinesthetic: Related to the movement and awareness of the body.
auditory: Related to the sense of hearing.
facilitators: People who make a process easier.

From the time they're four or five (or even younger) to the time they're eighteen, people spend a lot of time in school. Whether you love school, dread going to classes, or fall somewhere in between these extremes, chances are you will encounter at least one teacher during this time who makes a bigger impression on you than any other teacher. Perhaps it is a teacher who finally got you to understand that difficult algebra concept, or the teacher/coach who worked with you to improve your free throw. It's the teacher who helps you believe in yourself more than you ever did before, the teacher who opens a door for you somehow (even if the door is only in your own mind).

The education children and young adults receive in school helps shape their future lives, and teachers shape this education. Teachers not only provide access to intellectual knowledge, but they also foster character development and social skills. At every level of education, teachers provide the tools and the environment for their students to develop into responsible adults.

> **Did You Know?**
> In the United States, on average, by the time a student graduates from high school, he or she has probably spent about 14,472 hours in school!

CHOOSING THE RIGHT CAREER

The young adults of today will be the job force of tomorrow, so choosing a career that will best fit with the needs of the changing world will be important to job satisfaction and a successful life. With the vast array of career and job options, young adults need to understand which work will be the best match for their interests, talents, goals, and personality types. If you are ready for a challenging but extremely valuable career—one that will help mold future generations—a career as a teacher might be right for you.

Certain job industries are expected to gain importance within the early decades of the twenty-first century. The opportunities and the projected job growth for a teaching career will vary, depending on the type of teacher you wish to become. The United States Bureau of Labor Statistics divides teaching into a number of different categories: preschool; kindergarten, elementary, middle, and secondary; postsecondary; *vocational*; and special education. For all these categories, employment is expected to grow by an average of 14.6 percent through 2018, which is faster than the average projected growth of 11 percent for all occupations during that same time. The only teachers for which employment is predicted to grow at a slower than average rate are vocational teachers. Therefore, most teachers can expect to have good job opportunities over the next decade.

What Do Teachers Do?

To understand teaching and the importance of teachers, it is probably best to start by discussing the concept of learning. What does it mean to learn something? How do we learn? Does everyone learn the same way?

To learn is simply to gain new knowledge or skills, either through experience, through individual study, by being taught, or most often, by some combination of these three methods. These different learning styles can also be thought of as learning by touch, learning by seeing, or learning by listening.

Learning by experience or touch involves a physical involvement in the learning process. Much of what you learned as a baby or toddler was experiential in nature. For example, you probably learned what hot and cold meant by experiencing the temperatures for yourself. Your parents probably told you that their coffee was hot, and you may have seen your mother blowing on her coffee before sipping it, but most toddlers and young children won't understand what these things mean until they experience it for themselves, a style of learning known formally as *tactile-kinesthetic* learning.

Learning via study or seeing is to learn by reading about something, or by watching someone else. If you see your brother touch a hot stove and get burnt, and never touch a hot stove yourself because you do not want to get burnt as well, then you have learned by study. This ability to gain new knowledge by seeing is known as visual learning.

Learning by being taught or through listening is to gain a new skill or new knowledge because another person tells you about it. If all you needed to learn about the hot stove was from what your mother told you, then you learned by being taught. Because this style of learning involves listening as a key element, it is also known as *auditory* learning.

These three learning styles not only apply to young children but also to older students and adults. Everyone has a different type of learning style—auditory, visual, or tactile-kinesthetic. The challenge for teachers is to help students with a wide variety of learning styles all gain the same new information and skills.

Teachers act as *facilitators* or coaches, using lectures or one-on-one instruction to help students learn and apply concepts in various subjects. Teachers plan, evaluate, and assign lessons; prepare, administer, and grade tests; and maintain classroom discipline. They also observe student behavior and performance, and then use this to evaluate the student's progress and potential. Teachers also grade assignments and tests, prepare final grades or report cards, and meet with parents, school staff, and/or students to discuss academic progress or personal problems.

To help the widest variety of students and learning styles, teachers must be able to adapt their methods not only to each

Traditional classroom education has a teacher standing in front of the room giving a lecture. This may not be the best learning environment for every student.

new class, but also to each individual student within a classroom. Many teachers use visual aids or props to help students understand abstract concepts, solve problems, and develop critical thinking skills. For example, an elementary school teacher might teach math concepts by playing board games. As the students get older, teachers move to more sophisticated approaches, such as demonstrating science experiments, and computers are now common learning aids at all levels of education. Teachers

At all grade levels, teachers need to be able to adapt their teaching style for each student in their class.

Computers in the Classroom

In the modern classroom, computers play an important role in the education teachers provide. Computers and the Internet offer a wealth of educational opportunities if teachers know how best to use them in the classroom. For example, through the Internet, students can communicate with other students anywhere in the world, allowing them to share experiences and viewpoints. Students can use the Internet for individual research projects and to gather information. However, teachers need to familiarize themselves with the technology and carefully instruct students on the correct way to access reliable information online.

Computers play a role in other classroom activities as well, from solving math problems to learning a new language. Teachers also use computers to prepare and give presentations, record grades, or perform other organizational tasks. Teachers must continually update their skills so that they can use the latest technology in the classroom.

From a young age children are using computers at home and at school. Teachers need to understand available technology and teach their students how to use computers to improve their education.

also encourage teamwork by having students work in groups to discuss and solve problems together. Problem solving, use of technology, and the ability to interact and work with other people are all skills that will prepare students for continued success in school, but also success later in life.

Teachers also have to be able to work with students from varied ethnic, racial, and religious backgrounds. With growing minority populations in most parts of the country, it is important for teachers to be able to effectively teach a diverse student population. Some schools offer training to help teachers enhance their awareness and understanding of different cultures, and to learn how to address the needs of all students, regardless of their cultural backgrounds.

In addition to all of their teaching-based classroom responsibilities, teachers oversee study halls and homerooms, supervise extracurricular activities, and accompany students on field trips. They may identify students who have physical or mental problems and help these students get the additional support they need. Secondary school teachers might also counsel students in choosing courses, colleges, and careers.

WORK ENVIRONMENT

A teacher's work environment varies with different types of teachers—an elementary school teacher is likely to have a classroom of his own, while a college professor will move from lecture hall to lecture hall depending on the classes she is assigned each semester. At every level of education, seeing students develop new skills and knowledge can be very rewarding. However, a

What Kind of Person Are You?

Career-counseling experts know that certain kinds of people do best in certain kinds of jobs. John L. Holland developed the following list of personality types and the kinds of jobs that are the best match for each type. See which one (or two) are most like you. The more you understand yourself, the better you'll be able to make a good career plan for yourself.

- **Realistic personality**: This kind of person likes to do practical, hands-on work. He or she will most enjoy working with materials that can be touched and manipulated, such as wood, steel, tools, and machinery. This personality type enjoys jobs that require working outdoors, but he or she does NOT enjoy jobs that require a lot of paperwork or close teamwork with others.

- **Investigative personality**: This personality type likes to work with ideas. He or she will enjoy jobs that require lots of thinking and researching. Jobs that require mental problem solving will be a good fit for this personality.

- **Artistic personality**: This type of person enjoys working with forms, designs, and patterns. She or he likes jobs that require self-expression—and that don't require following a definite set of rules.

- **Social personality**: Jobs that require lots of teamwork with others, as well as teaching others, are a good match for this personality type. These jobs often involve helping others in some way.

- **Enterprising personality**: This person will enjoy planning and starting new projects, even if that involves a degree of risk-taking. He or she is good at making decisions and leading others.

- **Conventional personality**: An individual with this type of personality likes to follow a clear set of procedures or routines. He or she doesn't want to be the boss but prefers to work under someone else's leadership. Jobs that require working with details and facts (more than ideas) are a good fit for this personality.

teacher can also get frustrated if she is dealing with unmotivated, unruly, or disrespectful students. As with any job, teachers may experience job-related stress.

If you decide on a career as a teacher, be aware that many teachers work more than the normal forty hours a week. Teachers arrive at school before their students, stay later in the day, and often may bring work, such as lesson plans or grading, home at night or on weekends. The long summer break that seems so appealing is often filled with another job, teaching summer classes, or continuing education. Of course, many teachers do use their break to travel or pursue personal interests.

They may forget what you said but they will never forget how you made them feel.

—Carol Buchner

ABOUT THE QUOTE

Teaching is a career where your belief in your students will be far more powerful than even the most effective techniques and skills. We always remember people who bring out the best in us, and we learn best when we believe in ourselves. Are you able to see what is best in people? Can you share your vision?

CHAPTER 2
TYPES OF TEACHERS

WORDS TO KNOW

curriculum: The planned course of study for a school.

motor skills: Complex muscle and nerve interaction that produce movement of the body; fine motor skills are small movements like writing, while gross motor skills are large movements like walking.

phonics: A method of teaching children to read that relates letters or groups of letters with sounds.

seminar: A class in which a teacher and a small group of students learn topics through discussion.

remedial: Those programs and teaching methods that are intended to help students achieve improvements in their school work.

inclusive: Programs that bring together students of different physical and mental abilities in a classroom atmosphere of respect for and appreciation of their differences.

There are many different types of teachers, ranging from preschool teachers to college professors. In addition, at some levels of education, teachers specialize in a certain subject area, such as mathematics, English, or one of the sciences. These subject areas become more specialized as the educational level gets higher.

The type of teacher you become should be based on your academic interests, your personality, and your talents. If you dislike young children, a career as a preschool teacher is probably not going to be a good fit! Consider why you are interested in teaching: do you want to learn as much as you can about a certain topic and then pass that knowledge onto other people—or are you more interested in helping students with physical or intellectual disabilities be successful? A brief introduction of what each type of teacher does might help you narrow your choices.

Preschool Teachers

Preschool teachers nurture, teach, and care for children, usually ages three to five, who have not yet entered kindergarten. They do so through a *curriculum* that covers various areas of child development, such as *motor skills*, social and emotional development, and language development. Preschool teachers also introduce children to reading and writing, arts, science, and social studies. They use games, music, artwork, films, books, computers, and other tools to teach these concepts and skills.

Children at this age learn mainly through investigation, experience, play, and formal teaching. Preschool teachers use play, storytelling, rhyming, and playacting to further language and vocabulary development. Social skills are developed as the children learn to play together and share toys. Scientific and mathematical concepts are introduced in games. An approach that includes small and large group activities, one-on-one instruction, and learning through creative activities such as art, dance, and music, works best for preschool children. Concepts such as letters, *phonics*, numbers, and science are introduced at this level to prepare students for kindergarten.

KINDERGARTEN, ELEMENTARY, MIDDLE, AND SECONDARY TEACHERS

When people think of teachers, they are probably thinking about a teacher in this category. Kindergarten and elementary school teachers play a vital role in the development of young children. Middle school teachers expand on an elementary education, and help guide their students through years of great transition physically and emotionally. Secondary or high school teachers delve deeper into academic subjects, prepare students for college, and provide guidance to students preparing to enter the job force.

Preschool teachers spend a lot of time "playing" with their students. This playtime is used to introduce concepts the children will need to know for kindergarten.

KINDERGARTEN TEACHERS

Kindergarten teachers introduce children, usually ages five to six, to mathematics, language, science, and social studies. They use games, music, artwork, films, books, computers, and other methods to teach basic skills.

Like preschool teachers, kindergarten teachers use play and hands-on teaching, but academics gain additional importance in kindergarten classrooms. Letter recognition, phonics, numbers, and awareness of nature and science are standard concepts taught in kindergarten.

ELEMENTARY TEACHERS

Elementary teachers teach students usually ranging in age from six to eleven. Most elementary school teachers instruct one grade level, and one class of children in several subjects, such as mathematics, reading and writing, science, and social studies. In some schools, a teacher may teach one special subject—usually music, art, reading, science, arithmetic, or physical education—to students of all grade-levels.

MIDDLE SCHOOL AND SECONDARY SCHOOL TEACHERS

Middle school teachers and secondary school teachers work with students ages twelve to eighteen. These teachers explore subjects in more depth, introduce new subjects, and expose students to more information about the world. Middle and secondary teachers specialize in a specific subject, such as English, Spanish, mathematics, history, or biology.

Real Life Teacher

In 2008, Keil Hileman was honored by the United States Department of Education as a Teaching Ambassador Fellow. This program was created to honor outstanding teachers and to help these teachers share their expertise with other educators.

Mr. Hileman feels he was destined to become a teacher, but it took him a while to learn this about himself. He began his education studying engineering, and only discovered his love for teaching after taking an introduction to education course. He changed his education path and enrolled in a five-year education program at the University of Kansas. He earned a Bachelor's degree and a Master's degree in education, and is currently working on his doctorate in instructional technologies.

He has taught 6th and 8th grade history since 1994, as well as coaching volleyball, basketball, and track, and leading the math team. He finds other opportunities to teach—he leads an archaeology class at a local community college, a history of nursing course at the University of Missouri, and a teacher re-certification course at another nearby university. He just loves to teach!

"I have worked in many different jobs and educational situations, but nothing ever felt as amazing as teaching. Teaching is in my heart and soul."

(From www2.ed.gov/programs/teacherfellowship/fellows/hileman.html)

Postsecondary Teachers

Postsecondary teachers instruct students in a wide variety of academic and vocational subjects beyond the high school level. Postsecondary teachers include college and university faculty, postsecondary career and technical education teachers, and graduate teaching assistants. In addition to teaching, postsecondary teachers, particularly those at four-year colleges and universities, perform a significant amount of research in the subject they teach, keep up with new developments in their field, publish their research, and may consult with government, business, nonprofit, and community organizations.

Job opportunities are expected to be very good for postsecondary teachers. This is due to the increasing numbers of students enrolling in college—in 2009 a record 18.4 million students attended 2-year or 4-year colleges!

College and university faculty makes up the majority of post-secondary teachers. Faculty is usually organized into departments based on academic subject. They typically teach several related courses in their subject. A mathematics professor, for example, might teach courses in algebra, calculus, and statistics. Faculty may instruct undergraduate or graduate students or both. Class size and type varies by course; a professor may go from lecturing several hundred students in a large hall for one class to leading a small *seminar* for another. Professors prepare lectures, assignments, and laboratory experiments; grade exams and papers; and advise and work with students individually. In universities, they also supervise graduate students' teaching and research.

SPECIAL EDUCATION TEACHERS

Special education teachers work with children and youth who have a variety of disabilities. A small number of special education teachers work with students with severe disabilities, primarily teaching them life skills and basic literacy. However, most special education teachers work with children with mild to moderate disabilities, using or modifying the general education curriculum to meet the child's individual needs and providing required *remedial* instruction. Most special education teachers instruct students at the preschool, elementary, middle, and secondary school level, although some work with infants and toddlers.

Some of the types of disabilities that might qualify students for special education programs are learning disabilities, speech

IDEA

The Individuals with Disabilities Education Act (IDEA) is a law ensuring services to children with disabilities throughout the nation. IDEA governs how states and public agencies provide early intervention, special education, and related services to more than 6.5 million eligible infants, toddlers, children, and youth with disabilities.

or language impairments, intellectual disability, emotional disturbance, hearing impairments, visual impairments, or autism. Early identification of a child with special needs is important, because early intervention is essential in educating children with disabilities.

Special education teachers help to develop an Individualized Education Program (IEP) for each student receiving special education. The IEP sets personalized goals for the student, and is tailored to that student's needs and abilities. When appropriate, the program includes a transition plan to prepare students for middle school or high school or, in the case of older students, a job or postsecondary study. Teachers review the IEP with the student's parents, school psychologist, school administrators, and the student's general education teachers. Teachers work closely with parents to inform them of their children's progress and suggest techniques to promote learning outside of school.

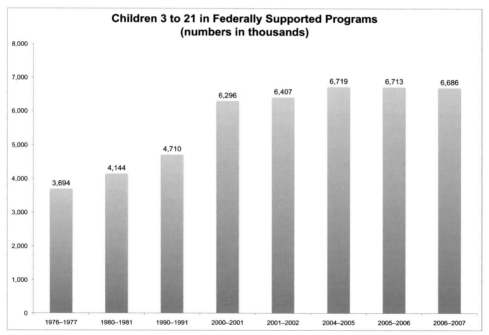

The signing of the first special education law in 1975 made it the right of every child with a disability to receive a free and appropriate public education. Since then, the numbers of children receiving special education under federal programs has increased almost every year.

Special education teachers and general education teachers increasingly work together in general education classrooms. Special education teachers help general educators adapt curriculum materials and teaching techniques to meet the needs of students with disabilities. They coordinate the work of teachers, teacher assistants, and related personnel, such as therapists and social workers, to meet the individualized needs of the student within *inclusive* special education programs. A large part of a special education teacher's job involves communicating and coordinating with others involved in the child's well-being, including parents, social workers, school psychologists, occupational and physical therapists, school administrators, and other teachers.

VOCATIONAL TEACHERS

Vocational education teachers, commonly called career and technical education (CTE) teachers or career-technology teachers, instruct and train students to work in a wide variety of fields. Career and technical education courses train students to enter a particular career and prepare them for the world of work.

Career and technical teachers in middle and secondary schools may be introducing students to a trade or skill for the first time. Additional responsibilities of middle and secondary school teachers may include providing career guidance and helping with job placement.

Vocational teachers may teach in regular middle or secondary schools, in vocational institutes, or in regional CTE centers that serve students from many districts who come for half-days.

If You Have a Social Personality...

Teaching is an ideal field for you to pursue. Being a teacher will give you many opportunities to help people who need you. Since you're genuinely and warmly interested in people, as a teacher you will be constantly interested in your career—and that's a good thing! You probably don't enjoy using machines and tools, and they're not likely to be a part of most teachers' professional lives (except for vocational teachers).

If You Have a Realistic Personality...

You might like to teach at a vocational school, where you can use practical tools and your mechanical know-how to teach students trades.

Don't try to fix the students, fix ourselves first. The good teacher makes the poor student good and the good student superior. When our students fail, we, as teachers, too, have failed.

—Marva Colli

ABOUT THE QUOTE

As a teacher you will need to remember that it is your job to find ways to make learning happen. Just as a doctor finds some patients easier to heal than others, some students will be easier to teach than others, but your job will remain the same. Helping students learn, regardless of the challenges, is something you will begin to learn during your training— and you will continue to learn during your entire career as a teacher.

CHAPTER 3
EDUCATION AND TRAINING

WORDS TO KNOW

bachelor's degree: The degree given to a student who completes four years of undergraduate studies; also known as a baccalaureate degree.

internship: A period of time during which a student works, with or without pay, at an occupation to gain work experience.

accredited: Earned official authorization after certain standards are met.

master's degree: The degree awarded to a student who has completed at least one year of graduate study.

Board of Education: An appointed or elected committee that controls the school system in a town, city, county, or state.

doctoral degree: Also called a Doctor of Philosophy (PhD), the degree awarded to a student beyond a master's degree, after the completion of at least three years of graduate study plus a dissertation; also known as a doctorate.

dissertation: A paper on original research in the candidate's major field of study.

distance learning: A method of study in which classes are taught or taken over the Internet, without the student needing to go to the location.

The amount of education and training you will need to work as a teacher varies, depending on the specific type of teaching that interests you. However, for most teaching careers, minimum training and education requirements will probably involve at least a *bachelor's degree*.

Kindergarten, Elementary, Middle, and Secondary Teachers

The traditional route to becoming a public school teacher involves completing a bachelor's degree from a teacher education program and then obtaining a license. However, many states now offer alternative ways for people who have a degree in other fields to earn a teaching license.

> **Did You Know?**
> Private school teachers do not have to be licensed but may still need a bachelor's degree.

Education programs for kindergarten and elementary school teachers include courses designed specifically for students preparing to teach. Among these courses are mathematics, physical science, social science, music, art, and literature, as well as education specific courses, such as philosophy of education, psychology of learning, and teaching methods. In addition, many programs now include classes on the use of computers and other technology in the classroom. Students studying to be secondary school teachers most often major in the subject they plan to teach, while also taking teacher preparation courses. Finally, most programs require students to perform a student-teaching *internship*, to allow the aspiring teacher to gain some teaching experience in front of a class.

Teacher education programs may be *accredited* by the National Council for Accreditation of Teacher Education and the Teacher Education Accreditation Council. Graduation from an accredited program is not necessary to become a teacher, but it may make fulfilling licensure requirements easier.

Most teaching programs require student teaching hours as part of their degree program. This gives the student the chance to practice his teaching skills in front of a real classroom.

Teaching License

All states require public school teachers to be licensed. Though specific requirements vary by state, all states require teachers to have a bachelor's degree, to complete a teacher training program, and to participate in supervised practice teaching. In addition, some states require that teachers get a *master's degree* within a certain amount of time after they start teaching. Usually a license is granted by a state *Board of Education* or a licensure advisory committee. Teachers may be licensed to teach special education (usually kindergarten through grade 12); the early childhood grades (usually preschool through grade 3); the elementary grades (grades 1 through 6 or 8); the middle grades (grades 5 through 8); a secondary-education subject area (usually grades 7 through 12); or a special subject, such as reading or music (usually grades kindergarten through 12).

Other Qualifications

In addition to being knowledgeable about the subjects they teach, teachers must have the ability to communicate, inspire trust and confidence, and motivate students, as well as understand the students' educational and emotional needs. Teachers must be able to recognize and respond to individual and cultural differences in students and employ different teaching methods that will result in higher student achievement. They should be organized, dependable, patient, and creative. Teachers also must be able to work cooperatively and communicate effectively with other teachers, support staff, parents, and members of the community.

Changed Your Mind?

What do you do if you get all the way through college with a degree in physics, but you suddenly realize that you really want to be a teacher—do you have to start all over again? No, you don't. Luckily, all states now offer alternative licensure programs for teachers who have a bachelor's degree in the subject they want to teach, but who lack the necessary education courses required for a teaching license. Many of these alternative licensure programs are designed to ease shortages of teachers in certain subjects, such as mathematics and the sciences. Other programs provide teachers for urban and rural schools that traditionally have difficulty filling positions.

These alternative licensure programs are intended to attract recent college graduates who did not complete education programs as well as people changing from another career to teaching. In some programs, individuals begin teaching quickly under provisional licensure under the close supervision of experienced educators while taking education courses outside school hours. If they progress satisfactorily, they receive regular licensure after working for one or two years. In other programs, college graduates who do not meet licensure requirements take only those courses they lack and then become licensed. This approach may only take one or two semesters of full-time study. The coursework for alternative certification programs often leads to a master's degree.

attain professional certification in order to demonstrate competency beyond that required for a license. The National Board for Professional Teaching Standards offers a voluntary national certification. All states recognize national certification, and many states and school districts provide special benefits to teachers who earn this certification. Benefits typically include a higher salary, reimbursement for continuing education, and the ability to carry a license from one state to another.

Most states have tenure laws that prevent public school teachers from being fired without just cause and due process. Teachers may obtain tenure after they have satisfactorily completed a probationary period of teaching, normally three years. Tenure does not absolutely guarantee a job, but it does provide some security.

Postsecondary Teachers

If you are interested in a career as a college professor, be prepared for a long educational commitment. Four-year colleges and universities usually require candidates for full-time, tenure-track positions to hold a *doctoral degree*. Doctoral programs take an average of six years of full-time study beyond the bachelor's degree, including time spent completing a master's degree and a *dissertation*. Some programs, such as those in the humanities, may take longer to complete; others, such as those in engineering, usually are shorter.

Doctoral candidates specialize in a subfield of a discipline and also take general courses covering the entire discipline. Programs typically include twenty or more increasingly specialized courses and seminars, plus comprehensive examinations in all major areas of the field.

In two-year colleges, master's degree holders fill most full-time teaching positions. However, in certain fields where there may be more applicants than available jobs, institutions can be more selective in their hiring practices. In these fields, master's degree holders may be passed over in favor of candidates holding PhDs. Many two-year institutions increasingly prefer job applicants to have some teaching experience or experience with *distance learning*. Preference also may be given to job applicants with multiple master's degrees, especially at smaller institutions, because they can teach more subjects.

If You Have an Investigative Personality. . .

You might enjoy teaching math or science at the high school or college level. Science and math professors at universities are expected to continue their own research, as well as teach, and you will likely find this part of your job a particularly good match for you skills and interests.

A teacher affects eternity; he can never tell where his influence stops.

—Henry Brooks Adams

CHAPTER 4
RELATED OCCUPATIONS
IN EDUCATION

A re you interested in a career in education, but not sure you want to be a teacher? There are many other job opportunities besides teaching available in the education world. And, with the alternative licensure programs in most states, you can always decide that teaching is the right choice for you, even if you start down an educational track to be something else.

You probably know just from the experience of going to school that there are other staff people besides teachers who work in the school and work with students. Some of these include teacher assistants, child-care workers, administrators, librarians, and counselors.

Teacher Assistants

Teacher assistants provide support for teachers, allowing teachers more time for lesson planning and teaching. They support and assist children in learning class material using the teacher's lesson plans, providing students with more one-on-one attention than the teacher is able to provide. Teacher assistants also supervise students in the cafeteria, schoolyard, and hallways, or on field trips; they record grades, set up equipment, and help prepare materials for instruction. Teacher assistants also are called teacher aides or instructional aides.

Many teacher assistants work extensively with special education students. As schools become more inclusive and *integrate* special education students into general education classrooms, teacher assistants in both general education and special education classrooms increasingly assist students with disabilities. They attend to the physical needs of students with disabilities, including feeding, teaching grooming habits, and assisting students riding the school bus. They also provide personal attention to students with other special needs, such as those who speak English as a second language and those who need remedial education.

Child-Care Workers

Child-care workers provide care for babies, toddlers, and young children who have not yet entered kindergarten. They also super-

Coaching

Coaching is a type of teaching applied to sports. Many former athletes choose to pursue a career as a coach so that they can stay active in the sport they love. Coaches in middle schools or high schools are usually teachers of academic subjects who supplement their income by coaching part time. College coaches, on the other hand, consider coaching a full-time discipline and may be away from home frequently as they travel to competitions and to scout and recruit prospective players.

vise older children before and after school. These workers play an important role in children's development by caring for them when their parents are at work or are away for other reasons or when the parents place their children in care to help them socialize with children their age. In addition to taking care of children's health, safety, and nutrition, child care workers organize activities and teach curricula that stimulate children's physical, emotional, intellectual, and social growth.

Child-care workers generally are classified into three different groups based on where they work: private household workers, who care for children at the children's homes; family child-care providers, who care for children in the providers' homes; and child-care workers who work at child-care centers, which include Head Start, Early Head Start, full-day and part-day preschool, and other early childhood programs. Most child-care jobs require a high school or a two-year degree.

If you are knowledgeable about a sport and love to share that information, then coaching might be a good career option. Many high school coaches also teach an academic subject.

Education Administrators

Education administrators provide leadership and manage the day-to-day activities in schools, preschools, day-care centers, and colleges and universities. Most of these positions require an additional administrators' certification on top of a teaching certification.

Education administrators set educational standards and establish policies and procedures required to achieve them. They also supervise managers, support staff, teachers, counselors, librarians, coaches, and other employees. They develop academic programs, monitor students' educational progress, train and motivate teachers and other staff, manage career counseling and other student services, administer recordkeeping, prepare budgets, and perform many other duties. They also handle relations with parents, prospective and current students, employers, and the community. In a smaller organization such as a small day-care center, one administrator may handle all or many of these functions. In universities or large school systems, responsibilities are divided among many administrators.

School Superintendents

The school superintendent is the only employee hired directly by the school board and serves as the chief executive officer of the board with general supervision of the school system. This is the position that has the most authority (and makes the most money) in public school districts. The superintendent is not a member of the school board itself but serves as the professional educational adviser to the board. The superintendent is hired to provide professional educational advice on policy development and implements the policies the board adopts.

The job description calls for the performance of the following duties: preparing the agenda for each meeting; preparing the annual budget for board consideration; preparing and submitting state and federal applications and reports; recommending the appointment and termination of all personnel; and maintaining a continuous study of the school's current problems. Other duties include keeping board members informed about the needs of the

School principals are sometimes scary for young students, since the "principal's office" is where you are sent to be disciplined. Most principals, though, are friendly, caring individuals who just want the best for their students and schools.

district and about school operations and programs; providing for the continuous improvement of all facets of school district operations, especially as it relates to teaching and learning; encouraging long-range and strategic planning; ensuring that professional development opportunities are available for district employees; developing a public relations program; assuring that all decisions are made with the best interests of students in mind.

PRINCIPALS

Educational administrators who manage elementary, middle, and secondary schools are called principals. They set the academic tone of the school and work with teachers to develop and maintain curriculum standards, and to establish performance goals and objectives. Principals hire and evaluate teachers and other staff, visit classrooms, observe teaching methods, review instructional objectives, and examine learning materials.

ASSISTANT PRINCIPALS

Assistant principals aid the principal in the overall administration of the school. Some assistant principals hold the position for only a few years, with the ultimate goal of advancing to a principal position, while others are assistant principals throughout their careers. They are primarily responsible for scheduling student classes and ordering textbooks and supplies. They also coordinate transportation, custodial, cafeteria, and other support services. They usually handle student discipline and attendance problems, social and recreational programs, and matters of health and safety.

College and University Administrators

In colleges and universities, provosts, also known as chief academic officers, assist presidents, make faculty appointments and tenure decisions, develop budgets, and establish academic policies and programs. With the assistance of academic deans and deans of faculty, provosts also direct and coordinate the activities of deans of individual colleges and chairpersons of academic departments. Fundraising is the chief responsibility of the director of development and at many schools is an essential part of the job for all administrators.

Department Heads

College or university department heads or chairpersons are in charge of departments that specialize in particular fields of study, such as English, biological science, or mathematics. In addition to teaching, they coordinate schedules of classes and teaching assignments; propose budgets; recruit, interview, and hire applicants for teaching positions; evaluate faculty members; encourage faculty development; serve on committees; and perform other administrative duties. In overseeing their departments, chairpersons must consider and balance the concerns of faculty, administrators, and students.

School Counselors

School counselors work in at all levels of education to help students understand and deal with social, behavioral, and personal problems. Their jobs require a specific certification that usually requires a master's degree. These counselors emphasize preventive and developmental counseling to improve students' lives and to help prevent problems from getting worse. Counselors also try to identify cases of *domestic abuse* and other family problems that might affect a student's development.

Elementary school counselors observe children during classroom and play activities, evaluate whether they have any special

A librarian is no longer just responsible for books. Librarians are now known as "information professionals," and it is their responsibility to help students access information not only in books, but also in magazines, in audio and visual media, and on the Internet.

needs, and confer with their teachers and parents about any concerns. Counselors work with teachers and administrators to make sure that the school curriculum addresses both the academic and the developmental needs of students.

High school counselors mainly help students with the transition to life after high school. If the student is planning to go on to college, the counselor will help with college applications, admission requirements, choice of major, and financial aid applications. They also advise students who plan to go into trade or technical schools, or *apprenticeship* programs. Finally counselors help prepare students who plan to enter the work force right out of school. They help these students find job opportunities, and teach them job search skills, such as resume writing and interviewing techniques.

LIBRARIANS

Librarians, often called information professionals, help people find information and use it effectively for personal and professional purposes. Their jobs also require a specific certification that usually requires a master's degree. They must have knowledge of a wide variety of scholarly and public information sources and be able to follow trends related to publishing, computers, and the media to oversee the selection and organization of library materials. School librarians, known as school media specialists, help students access information in printed media, as well as on the Internet. School librarians also teach students how to use the library and how to do research in general.

If You Have a Conventional Personality. . .

You might like being a teacher's assistant, where your ability to follow directions in an orderly way will be an asset to you.

If You Have an Enterprising Personality. . .

You might enjoy becoming a principal or superintendent in a school. In a job like this you would have plenty of chances to let your energetic, sociable, and ambitious nature shine, and your abilities to be a leader would make you effective with both students and teachers. Remember, though, that becoming a principal usually requires that you have experience first working as a teacher. You will need to work your way up from being a teacher to being an assistant principal (after getting your administrator's certificate) to being a principal, and finally, to being a school superintendent.

To teach is to learn twice.

—Joseph Joubert

ABOUT THE QUOTE

If you decide to pursue a career in teaching, you will be committing yourself to a life of learning. The best teachers never stop expanding their minds. They enjoy the thrill of discovery alongside their students. Does this sound like the right career for you?

CHAPTER 5
THE FUTURE OF TEACHING

WORDS TO KNOW

bilingual education: Teaching programs conducted in two languages, often with students for whom English is their second language.

prospective: An option that is being considered, and that is reasonably likely to happen.

In general, the job outlook for teaching is expected to be good. Some types of teachers will have greater job opportunities and employment growth than others. Job prospects will be best for teachers in high-demand fields, such as mathematics, science, and *bilingual education*, as well as for teachers willing to take jobs in less desirable urban or rural school districts.

Employment of kindergarten, elementary, middle, and secondary school teachers is expected to grow by 13 percent between 2008 and 2018, which is slightly faster than the average of 11 percent for all occupations. The teachers with the fastest projected employment growth over this time period are preschool teachers at 19 percent and special education teachers at 17 percent.

Through 2018, overall student enrollments in elementary, middle, and secondary schools—a key factor in the demand for teachers—are expected to rise more slowly than in the past, but projected enrollments will vary by region. Enrollment in preschool programs is also expected to rise more slowly than in the past, but because of an increased emphasis on early childhood education and full-day programs in some areas will increase the demand for preschool teachers. In general, teachers who are willing to move to where the jobs are, who get National Certification (so they can teach in multiple states), and who obtain licensure in more than one subject are likely to have a distinct advantage in finding a job.

Special education teachers can look forward to a faster than average employment growth because the number of students requiring special education services is growing. Improvements in diagnosis have allowed learning disabilities to be recognized at earlier ages. In addition, legislation emphasizing equal standards of training and employment for individuals with disabilities and educational reforms requiring higher standards for graduation have increased the demand for special education services. Also, the percentage of foreign-born special education students is expected to grow as teachers become more adept in recognizing disabilities in these populations. Finally, more parents are expected to seek special services for children who have difficulty meeting the new, higher standards required of students.

Postsecondary teachers have a projected employment growth of 15 percent over the next decade. This expected growth is due mostly to increases in college and university enrollment over the next decade. This enrollment growth stems mainly from the expected increase in the population of eighteen- to twenty-four-year-olds, and from the increasing number of high school graduates who choose to attend these institutions. Also, adults returning to college to enhance their career prospects, to update their skills, or to change careers will also continue to create new opportunities for postsecondary teachers, particularly at community colleges and other institutions that cater to working adults.

WHERE WILL THE JOBS BE?

Job opportunities should be better in inner cities and rural areas than in suburban districts. Many inner cities—often characterized by overcrowded, ill-equipped schools and higher-than-average poverty rates—and rural areas—characterized by their remote location and relatively low salaries—have difficulty attracting and keeping enough teachers. Also, many school districts (despite location) have trouble hiring qualified teachers in some subject areas—most often mathematics, science (especially chemistry and physics), bilingual education, and foreign languages. Increasing enrollments of minorities, coupled with a shortage of minority teachers, should cause efforts to recruit minority teachers to intensify. Also, the number of non-English-speaking students will continue to grow, creating demand for bilingual teachers and for those who teach English as a second language. Job prospects are expected to be worse for those teaching specialties that have enough qualified teachers, such as general elementary education, physical education, and social studies.

In the next decade, science and mathematics teachers will be more in demand than general education teachers. This science teacher from Compton, California, is getting additional education in "green" energy from her mentor at the Lawrence Berkeley National Laboratory.

Planning for the Future

The information in this book is meant to be only an introduction to teaching and to some of the career opportunities available for teachers and other educators. If you think you are interested in one of these careers, it is never too early to start learning your options or to begin gaining experience.

• Speak to a school guidance counselor about your career plans, and get advice on the best educational path to help you achieve your goals.

• A guidance counselor might also help you find student jobs, internships, or other educational opportunities related to teaching in your area.

• A guidance counselor can also help you decide what area of teaching you might be best suited for, and what educational track will be right for you.

• Get a summer or a part-time job at a child-care center to get experience working with, caring for, and even teaching children.

• Volunteer as a coach as another way to gain experience teaching children.

• If postsecondary teaching interests you, find opportunities now to gain experience in your chosen subject. This will help you narrow your focus of study once in college.

Everything you do that is related to your interest in a teaching career will help guide you to the specialization for which you are most suited and will strengthen you in the eyes of *prospective* schools or employers.

If You Have a Creative Personality. . .

You might enjoy combining your artistic talents with teaching. Music and art teachers work at all levels of education. Many high schools and most colleges also have drama teachers—or if you enjoy creative writing, you might want to teach literature, fiction writing, or poetry at the college level, or teach high school English. Artistic and musical skills can also be particularly useful to preschool teachers. Your ability to think in original ways may help you to excel in many different kinds of teaching positions, including special education, since being able to think "outside the box" will help you to be an effective and interesting teacher who can adapt to each student's learning needs.

Further Reading

Heaton, J. Barrett, and Barrett Heaton. *Careers in Teaching.* New York: Rosen Publishing Group, 2005.

Hougan, Eric. *Road to Teaching: A Guide to Teacher Training, Student Teaching, and Finding a Job.* North Charleston, S.C.: BookSurge Publishing, 2008.

National Council for Accreditation of Teacher Education. *A Guide to College Programs in Teacher Preparation.* San Francisco, Calif.: Jossey-Bass, Inc., 1999.

Starkey, Lauren. *Change Your Career: Teaching as Your New Profession.* New York: Kaplan Publishing, 2007.

Stebleton, Michael, Michael Henle, and Connie Harris. *Hired! The Job-Hunting/Career-Planning Guide.* Upper Saddle River, N.J.: Prentice Hall, 2005.

Weimer, Maryellen. *Inspired College Teaching: A Career-Long Resource for Professional Growth.* San Francisco, Calif.: Jossey-Bass, Inc., 2010.

FIND OUT MORE ON THE INTERNET

Alternative Certificate Programs
www.teach-now.org

National Board Certification
www.nbpts.org

National Council for Accreditation of Teacher Education
www.ncate.org

Student Educational Resources
www.usa.gov/Citizen/Topics/Education_Training/Student_Resourc-
es.shtml

Teachers' Educational Resources
www.usa.gov/Citizen/Topics/Education_Training/Teacher_Resourc-
es.shtml

United States Department of Education
www2.ed.gov/teachers/landing.jhtml

DISCLAIMER
The websites listed on this page were active at the time of publication. The publisher is not responsible for websites that have changed their address or discontinued operation since the date of publication. The publisher will review and update the websites upon each reprint.

BIBLIOGRAPHY

Bureau of Labor Statistics. "Counselors," www.bls.gov/oco/ocos067. htm (10 May 2010).

Bureau of Labor Statistics. "Postsecondary," www.bls.gov/oco/ ocos066.htm (10 May 2010).

Bureau of Labor Statistics. "Preschool, Except Special Education," www.bls.gov/oco/ocos317.htm (8 May 2010).

Bureau of Labor Statistics. "Special Education," www.bls.gov/oco/ ocos070.htm (13 May 2010).

Bureau of Labor Statistics. "Teacher Assistants," www.bls.gov/oco/ ocos153.htm (13 May 2010).

Bureau of Labor Statistics. "Teachers—Kindergarten, Elementary, Middle, and Secondary," www.bls.gov/oco/ocos318.htm (8 May 2010).

Bureau of Labor Statistics. "Vocational Teachers," www.bls.gov/oco/ ocos358.htm (18 May 2010).

United States Department of Education. "Building the Legacy: IDEA 2004," idea.ed.gov (12 May 2010).

INDEX

Picture Credits

Creative Commons Attribution-ShareAlike 2.0 Generic
    freeloosedirt: pg. 46

Fotolia.com
    aceshot: pg. 32
    Andres Rodriguez: pg. 35
    AVAVA: pg. 40
    Johanna Goodyear: pg. 8
    John Johnson: pg. 44
    Lisa F. Young: pg. 49
    Lorraine Swanson: pg. 52
    Marc Dietrich: pg. 13
    Monika Adamczyk: pp. 20, 23
    Monkey Business: pg. 14
    Steven Pepple: pg. 16

Lawrence Berkeley National Laboratory: pg. 56

About the Author

Malinda Miller lives and works in upstate New York. After earning a graduate degree in anthropology, she found work at a small publisher, where she enjoys the opportunity to research and write on a variety of topics.

About the Consultant

Michael Puglisi is the director of the Department of Labor's Workforce New York One Stop Center in Binghamton, New York. He has also held several leadership positions in the International Association of Workforce Professionals (IAWP), a non-profit educational association exclusively dedicated to workforce professionals with a rich tradition and history of contributions to workforce excellence. IAWP members receive the tools and resources they need to effectively contribute to the workforce development system daily. By providing relevant education, timely and informative communication and valuable findings of pertinent research, IAWP equips its members with knowledge, information and practical tools for success. Through its network of local and regional chapters, IAWP is preparing its members for the challenges of tomorrow.